Sir Arthur

by Sunita Apte

illustrated by Chris Kotsakis

SCHOLASTIC INC.

New York Toronto London Auckland Sydney
Mexico City New Delhi Hong Kong Buenos Aires

Developed by Kirchoff/Wohlberg, Inc., in cooperation with Scholastic Inc.

Copyright © 2002 by Scholastic Inc.
All rights reserved. Published by Scholastic Inc. Printed in the U.S.A.
ISBN 0-439-35154-5
SCHOLASTIC and associated logos and designs are trademarks
and/or registered trademarks of Scholastic Inc.
8 9 10   24   09 08 07 06 05 04

THE MAN BEHIND SHERLOCK HOLMES

You may have heard of Sherlock Holmes. He is a famous detective who solves cases with his assistant, Dr. Watson. You may not know that Sherlock Holmes isn't a real person. He's a fictional character. A man named Arthur Conan Doyle made him up. Doyle was actually quite a character himself!

Arthur Conan Doyle was both a doctor and a writer. He was born in 1859 and grew up in Edinburgh, Scotland. In 1876, he went to medical school. There he met a man who would change his life. The man's name was Dr. Joseph Bell.

THE MODEL FOR SHERLOCK HOLMES

Dr. Bell was one of Conan Doyle's teachers. Conan Doyle was amazed at Dr. Bell's deductive skills. He was always very impressed at the way Dr. Bell could draw remarkable conclusions just from his observations about people.

Bell would often do this with new patients. For instance, he might say, "This patient is a left-handed shoemaker." To explain, he might say, "Look at this man's pants. The right leg is more worn out than the left. That's because he rests shoes on his right leg and hammers with his left hand."

Conan Doyle never forgot this amazing professor. He became the model for Sherlock Holmes.

SHERLOCK HOLMES IS BORN

Conan Doyle didn't really like being a doctor. What he liked to do was write. So he began writing in his spare time.

One day in 1886, Conan Doyle jotted down notes for a new story. It was to be a detective story called "A Tangled Skein." The story had two main characters. One was a detective named Sherrinford Holmes. The other was his assistant, Ormond Sacker.

As writers often do, Conan Doyle ended up changing the story a lot before he finished it. For one thing, he changed its name from "A Tangled Skein" to "A Study in Scarlet." For another, he changed the two main characters' names. Sherrinford Holmes became Sherlock Holmes. Ormond Sacker became Dr. Watson. The rest, as they say, is history.

"A Study in Scarlet" was the very first Sherlock Holmes story. Soon, Conan Doyle began writing more of them. Sherlock Holmes became very popular. Readers couldn't get enough of him.

Why was Sherlock Holmes so popular? There were many reasons. Readers liked the way Holmes figured things out. They also liked his friend, Dr. Watson. He was less interesting than Holmes, but he told the stories well.

Conan Doyle went on to write many stories about Sherlock Holmes. But he grew tired of the great detective. After 24 stories, he decided to kill Holmes off.

In the story "The Final Problem," Conan Doyle sent the detective to his death. He had Holmes die in a plunge from a waterfall.

Readers were unhappy to see Holmes die. They demanded that Conan Doyle bring the detective back. Eight years later, Conan Doyle gave in to readers' demands. He wrote more Sherlock Holmes stories.

First, Conan Doyle wrote about old cases that happened before Holmes died. Then Conan Doyle had Holmes reappear. It seems he had not really died after all!

CONAN DOYLE THE DETECTIVE

Conan Doyle himself played detective more than once. In two famous cases, he helped free innocent men who were in prison. He did it just as Holmes would have done. He investigated the facts.

The first case involved a man named George Edalji. Edalji was in prison for killing farm animals near his home. Conan Doyle thought that Edalji was innocent. So he studied all the facts in the case. He deduced that Edalji could not have done the crimes. His educated opinion helped to free Edalji.

The second case was a little harder. A man named Oscar Slater was in jail for murder. Again, Conan Doyle examined the facts. He concluded that Slater was innocent. He fought to have Slater freed. Finally Slater was released. He had spent 17 years in prison.

A RICH AND FAMOUS WRITER

Sherlock Holmes is Conan Doyle's most popular main character. But he is not the only one. Conan Doyle wrote many books and stories that weren't about Sherlock Holmes.

Some of them are about an eccentric, courageous explorer named Professor Challenger. The stories about Professor Challenger are science fiction. *The Lost World* is probably the best-known Professor Challenger story. In this book, the professor leads an expedition to an island filled with dinosaurs.

A lifetime of writing made Conan Doyle rich and famous. Even members of the British royal family were Sherlock Holmes fans. In 1902, the King of England made Conan Doyle a knight.

Conan Doyle died in 1930. Sherlock Holmes, however, is still popular with readers all over the world.

As you read this retelling of a Sherlock Holmes story, you will go on a case with the greatest detective of them all.

THE ADVENTURE OF THE SPECKLED BAND

Very early one morning I woke to find Sherlock Holmes standing by the side of my bed. I was surprised. He usually slept late.

"Many apologies for waking you so early, Watson," Holmes said. "But we have a new client, a young lady. She is awaiting us in the sitting room."

This was exciting news! I always loved getting a new case.

Moments later we entered the sitting room. "Good morning," Holmes said cheerfully to the young woman sitting there. "My name is Sherlock Holmes. This is my friend and associate, Dr. Watson. You must be tired, having come in by train early this morning."

"Have you been following me?" the woman asked, startled.

"No, but I see the second half of a return train ticket in your left hand," Holmes replied.

I smiled at this exchange. Holmes's powers of observation were really quite amazing.

Suddenly, the woman looked frightened. "Please, let me tell you my story," she begged.

"By all means, go ahead," Holmes said.

The woman began. "My name is Helen Stoner. My mother is dead. I live with my stepfather at Stoke Moran Manor in the county of Surrey. He brought up my twin sister Julia and I.

"My mother left quite an inheritance. Her will dictated that when my sister and I got married, we would each get some of it. That meant my stepfather would have less of the inheritance at his disposal.

"Two years ago my sister fell in love and decided to get married. My stepfather didn't object. But two weeks before the wedding, a terrible event occurred.

"It was night. My sister and I were preparing for bed. We were in my room.

"'Helen,' she asked, 'have you heard a strange whistle during the night lately?'

'No,' I answered. 'Why do you ask?'

"'Because the last few nights, a strange whistle has awakened me. I'm surprised you haven't heard it. You must sleep more deeply than I do. It's not really important, I guess.' Then Julia left me and went into her room.

"I had difficulty sleeping that night. Then, just before dawn, I heard a woman's terrified scream. I knew at once that it was my sister.

"I rushed into her room. I was horrified at what I found. Julia's face was white with terror. She shrieked, 'Helen! It was the band! The speckled band!' Then she pointed in the direction of my stepfather's room. She tried to say more, but began choking instead. I watched, in agony, as my beloved twin sister died. No one was ever able to figure out what caused her death."

"I am sorry for your loss," Holmes said gently. "But that was over two years ago. Why have you come to see me so long afterwards?"

"Well you see, I am about to be married. Since my sister died, I have been sleeping in her old room. Lately, I have also begun hearing a strange whistle at night. I am convinced someone is trying to kill me, too!"

"So you think your sister was murdered?" Holmes asked Helen.

"Yes, though I cannot prove it." Helen replied. "I don't know how someone would have gotten into her room. The windows are barred and Julia always locked her door at night. You may think I am crazy, but I live in fear."

"No," said Holmes thoughtfully, "You are wise to live in fear. It does seem that your sister was murdered. Someone may be trying to kill you, too. I think Dr. Watson and I should come out to Stoke Moran. We could take a look at your sister's room. Is there a time we can come when your stepfather will be away?"

"Yes, he will be away all day today," replied Helen. "Come out this afternoon."

That afternoon, Holmes and I arrived at Stoke Moran. The old manor house had fallen into a state of disrepair. Helen met us at the door. She led us down a long hallway into her sister's room. Holmes looked around.

"Indeed, Watson," he said. "If one examines the room it is evident that there is no other way into this room besides the door. Look, the windows have bars. No one could climb through them."

"Yes," I agreed. "It is all very mysterious."

Holmes said nothing for a few minutes. He was busy studying every inch of the room. Suddenly he pointed a finger up at the ceiling. "Look, there is a vent in the ceiling!" he cried. "Where does it go?"

"That vent goes into my stepfather's room," Helen replied. "It was put in a couple of years ago."

"Very interesting," Holmes mused. "I think perhaps it is time to see your stepfather's room."

Helen led us down the hall into the room next door. It was neat and empty. Against the wall, under the vent from Julia's room, was an old armchair. Next to the bed was a big iron safe.

"What does your stepfather keep in that safe?" asked Holmes.

"I don't know. I suppose papers and things."

"Perhaps," Holmes murmured. "I tell you what. I think Dr. Watson and I should spend the night in your room tonight. You can sleep elsewhere. But do not let your stepfather know we are here."

I sensed from the tone of his voice that Holmes had cracked the case. He knew the identity of the killer. I was eager to see what the night would bring.

That night, Holmes and I sat in the dark in Helen's room. We had to be absolutely still. I was sure he was waiting for something, but I knew not what it was.

Suddenly, we heard a low whistle. Immediately, Holmes sprang up and lit a match. He poked furiously at the vent with his cane.

"You see it, Watson," he yelled. "You see it?"

I could see nothing, but in the next moment a horrible scream came from the stepfather's room next door. We rushed over.

Helen's stepfather sat upright in the armchair. He made no sound or movement. Around his head was wound a peculiar yellow band. It was covered with brown speckles.

"The band! The speckled band!" whispered Holmes.

I took a step forward. In an instant the band began to move. I gasped. The band was a snake! Quickly, I took out my pistol and shot it.

"A swamp adder! cried Holmes. "The deadliest snake in India. Helen's stepfather died ten seconds after being bitten by it."

Later, Holmes explained how Helen's sister had been deviously murdered.

"You see, Helen's stepfather had trained the snake," he said. "He kept it in the safe and would let it out through the vent every night. Before morning he called it back with a whistle. That way, no one would ever see the snake or suspect a snakebite as being the cause of death. He did not want to lose Helen's or her sister's money. He devised what he thought was a very ingenious plan. Only it came back to bite him!"

Wasn't that fun? If you liked this story, then you should try another.